WATER TREATMENT PRACTICE EXAMS FOR GRADES 2&3

Copyright © 2019 by Joshua Armstrong

All rights reserved. This book or any portion thereof
may not be reproduced or used in any matter whatsoever
without the express written permission of the publisher
except for the use of brief quotations in a book review.

PREFACE

This book was made for people looking into taking the California water treatment operator certification exams, particularly for grade levels 2-3. If you are in a state other than California, you can still benefit from these questions; most other states will be very similar, if not identical. This book contains 2 full length practice exams with answer sheets in the back along with step by step solutions on how to solve the math problems. Each exam within this book contains 85 multiple choice questions and 15 math questions just like the real test. On exam day you get 3 hours to complete the exam and the math questions are worth double points. Try not to memorize the questions and answers but rather try to understand the concepts behind the questions which will better solidify your memory regarding these topics. The wording of these questions may differ slightly on the actual exam; hence why it is important to understand the concepts of the material.

Taking practice tests has been proven as a very effective study technique. To get the most out of this book, try to answer the questions to the best of your ability and if you get some wrong, look up and research the question and it's answer in order to better your understanding of the topic for the future.

I highly recommend reading the water treatment books volumes 1 & 2 offered by CSU Sacramento Office of Water Programs. Those books alone would definitely get you through grades 1-3 certification levels. I also highly recommend picking up a Cal Rural Water Association workbook. Their study guides are a great resource to have. Lastly, I'd also like to recommend the Introduction to Water Treatment: Handbook Edition from Amazon. It's a book that I wrote that goes over all the basic fundamentals that every water treatment operator should know before going into taking a test.

When test day comes, relax and take all the time that you need in order to answer your questions comfortably. Make sure to get a good night's sleep before test day and eat a good breakfast before you leave. All test taking really comes down to is if you put in the hours of studying beforehand or not. If you want it bad enough, you're going to have to work for it and find the time to put into it. A good baseline for a decent study schedule is at least 30 minutes a day. Try the best that you can, and good luck on your exam.

TABLE OF CONTENTS

Practice Exam #1..1

Practice Exam #2..19

Exam #1 Answer Sheet.. 39

Exam #2 Answer Sheet...47

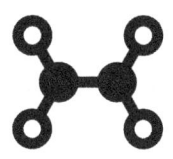

PRACTICE EXAM #1

1. Trihalomethanes are formed by the reaction of organic matter and
    a. Ammonia
    b. Oxygen
    c. Chlorine
    d. Lead

2. What is the log removal for viruses?
    a. 99.9%
    b. 99.99%
    c. 99%
    d. 9%

3. What test would an operator use in the field to take a chlorine residual?
    a. Amperometric Titration
    b. MPN
    c. NTU
    d. DPD

4. Cryptosporidium is what type of pathogen?
    a. Virus
    b. Protozoan
    c. Bacteria
    d. Radionuclide

5. Where on the pH scale is the water considered 'neutral'?
    a. 7
    b. 0
    c. 14
    d. 8.5

6. Where does the layer of anthracite coal go in a multi-media filter bed?
    a. Middle
    b. Bottom
    c. Top
    d. Mixed with other the layers of media

7. Direct filtration consists of the same processes of conventional filtration but excludes:
    a. Flash Mix
    b. Coagulation
    c. Flocculation
    d. Sedimentation

8. What happens at stage 4 of the breakpoint chlorination curve?
    a. Formation of chlororganics and chloramines
    b. Chlorine is destroyed by reducing compounds
    c. Free available chlorine residual is formed
    d. Chlororganics and chloramines are partly destroyed

9. Which is the correct order of processes in conventional filtration.
    a. flash mix, coagulation, flocculation, sedimentation, and filtration
    b. Coagulation, sedimentation, flocculation, flash mix, and filtration
    c. Flocculation, coagulation, flash mix, sedimentation, and filtration
    d. Filtration, sedimentation, flocculation, coagulation, and flash mix

10. Which of the following is a radionuclide?
    a. Ammonia
    b. Carbon dioxide
    c. Radon
    d. Cryptosporidium

11. Which of the following lowers pH?
    a. Lime
    b. Caustic soda
    c. Soda ash
    d. Carbon dioxide

12. Which of the following oxidants is not considered a disinfectant?
    a. Ozone
    b. Potassium Permanganate
    c. Chlorine
    d. Chlorine dioxide

13. What must the minimum chlorine residual leaving the treatment plant be?
    a. 4.0 mg/L
    b. 2.0 mg/L
    c. 0.4 mg/L
    d. 0.2 mg/L

14. What happens to the rate of head loss in a filter with media that is more uniform?
    a. Increases
    b. Decreases
    c. Stays the same
    d. Not affected

15. Which is a characteristic of chlorine gas?
    a. Greenish yellow color
    b. 2 1/2 times heavier than air
    c. Supports combustion
    d. All the above

16. What's the log removal for cryptosporidium?
    a. 99%
    b. 9%
    c. 99.9%
    d. 99.99%

17. Which two constituents cause hardness in the water?
    a. Iron and manganese
    b. Lead and copper
    c. Calcium and magnesium
    d. Ammonia and nitrites

18. Potassium permanganate causes what color if overdosed?
    a. Brown
    b. Black
    c. Blue
    d. Pink

19. What is a characteristic of a primary regulation/ standard?
    a. Does not pertain to things that affect health
    b. Things that directly affect health
    c. Applies only to the water's aesthetic concerns
    d. Regulations which are not mandatory

20. Which is considered a public water system?
    a. Has at least 15 service connections or serves at least 25 or more people for 60 days or more of the year.
    b. Has at least 15 service connections or serves at least 30 or more people for 60 days or more of the year.
    c. Has at least 30 service connections or serves at least 35 or more people for 60 days or more of the year.
    d. Has at least 15 service connections or serves at least 25 or more people for 30 days or more of the year.

21. Who enforces the water regulations?
    a. EPA
    b. Water system owner
    c. State
    d. Laboratory

22. What temperature do consumers like their water to be?
    a. 50-60 degrees
    b. 70-80 degrees
    c. 30-40 degrees
    d. 40-50 degrees

23. What is the main objective of a water treatment operator?
    a. Produce water at a reasonable cost
    b. Produce a safe drinking water
    c. Make as much revenue as possible
    d. Produce a subprime water

24. What is a pathogen?
    a. Virus
    b. Cryptosporidium
    c. Something able to cause disease
    d. All the above

25. Which is used as an indicator organism?
    a. Coliform
    b. Chloramine
    c. Nitrates
    d. Brilliant green bile

26. What is the concentration of chlorine gas?
    a. 12.5%
    b. 65%
    c. 34%
    d. 100%

27. Excessive growths of algae can produce what?
    a. Taste and odors
    b. Clear water
    c. Hardness
    d. Cavitation

28. What creates the vacuum required to operate a chlorinator?
    a. Wear rings
    b. Stuffing box
    c. Injector
    d. Rotameter

29. Tablets of ___ ___ are usually used to disinfect gravel packing:
    a. Sodium hypochlorite
    b. Chlorine gas
    c. Aluminum sulfate
    d. Calcium hypochlorite

30. What is the process of water moving from leaves and other plants to the atmosphere?
    a. Transpiration
    b. Precipitation
    c. Percolation
    d. Advection

31. If something in the water exceeds an MCL, who is responsible for notifying consumers?
    a. State
    b. Laboratory
    c. OSHA
    d. Water supplier

32. Reservoir ___ has the greatest impact on the effectiveness of copper sulfate.
    a. Dissolved oxygen
    b. Turnover
    c. Alkalinity
    d. Colloids

33. What is a confined aquifer?
    a. Body of water that is contained by two impermeable layers
    b. Body of water that has one layer open to atmospheric conditions
    c. River
    d. Lake

34. What is the top layer of a reservoir called?
    a. Hypolimnion
    b. Metalimnion
    c. Thermocline
    d. Epilimnion

35. What is the log removal for Giardia?
    a. 99.99%
    b. 99.9%
    c. 99%
    d. 9%

36. Chloramines are made from a combination of chlorine and what?
    a. UV
    b. Cryptosporidium
    c. Ammonia
    d. Nitrites

37. What is the best way of determining how much chlorine is left in a cylinder?
    a. Weigh the cylinder
    b. Tap the cylinder and listen to the sound
    c. Titration
    d. Looking at the rotameter

38. What is the most common solution feeder for liquid coagulants and coagulant aids?
    a. Turbine pump
    b. Centrifugal pump
    c. Volumetric feeder
    d. Metering pump

39. The disadvantage of ____ pumps is that they need periodic flexible tubing replacement.
    a. Piston
    b. Diaphragm
    c. Peristaltic
    d. Slaker

40. Which of the following is a groundwater source?
    a. Lake
    b. Well
    c. River
    d. Stream

41. Which of the following categories does bacteria belong to?
    a. Volatile inorganics
    b. Pesticides
    c. Dissolved
    d. Colloidal

42. How long does it take to neutralize the negative charges in a flash mixer?
    a. 1-2 seconds
    b. 15-45 minutes
    c. 45-60 minutes
    d. 4 hours

43. What would happen if a valve is closed too quickly?
    a. Cavitation
    b. Increased turbidity
    c. Water hammer
    d. Mudballs

44. Turbidity of settled water before its applied to the filter should be below _ to _ ntu.
    a. 0.3-0.4
    b. 1-2
    c. 4-5
    d. 5-10

45. Tube settlers are designed to:
    a. Increase the efficiency of sedimentation basins
    b. Be installed at 50-60 degree angles
    c. Increase settleable particulate removal in a smaller footprint
    d. All the above

46. What is used to protect the underdrain of a filter?
    a. Sand
    b. Anthracite
    c. Garnet
    d. Gravel

47. Complete destruction of all organisms in the water is called ___.
    a. Disinfection
    b. Sterilization
    c. Activation
    d. Ripening

48. When the total number of particulates increase in the first few minutes of running a filter after a backwash is called:
    a. Air binding
    b. Mudballs
    c. Filter ripening
    d. Surface wash

49. Which is a bacteria found in the intestinal tract of warm-blooded animals and in their waste?
    a. Coliform
    b. Algae
    c. Salmonella
    d. Legionella

50. Derivatives of methane in which three halogen atoms are substituted for three hydrogen atoms are called:
    a. Diatoms
    b. Trihalomethanes
    c. Hydrogen sulfide
    d. Ammonia

51. The annual quantity of water that can be taken from a source of supply over a period of time without depleting the source permanently is called:
    a. Safe yield
    b. Total yield
    c. Well drawdown
    d. Permeability

52. The biological layer on top of a slow sand filter is called:
    a. Hypolimnion
    b. Sand boil
    c. Schmutzdecke
    d. Organic precursor

53. What is typically the first layer of a reservoir to become anaerobic?
    a. Epilimnion
    b. Metalimnion
    c. Thermocline
    d. Hypolimnion

54. What test simulates coagulation and flocculation with different coagulant or polymer doses?
    a. MPM
    b. Most probable number
    c. Jar test
    d. DPD

55. A _____ sample is nearly identical in content and consistency to that of the larger body of water being sampled.
    a. Grab
    b. Representative
    c. Total
    d. Solid

56. The process of the addition of oxygen and removal of hydrogen from an element or compound is called:
    a. Reduction
    b. Oxidation
    c. Removing
    d. Addition

57. What kind of charge do coagulants have?
    a. Positive
    b. Negative
    c. Neutral
    d. Anionic

58. What are water sources that are rich in nutrients called?
    a. Oligotrophic
    b. Mesotrophic
    c. Littoral
    d. Eutrophic

59. What is a carcinogen?
    a. Nutrient
    b. Coagulant
    c. Substance capable of causing cancer
    d. Disinfectant

60. Which is the correct order of media in a multi-media filter bed from top to bottom?
    a. Gravel, garnet, sand, anthracite
    b. Sand, anthracite, garnet, gravel
    c. Anthracite, sand, garnet, gravel
    d. Anthracite, sand, gravel, garnet

61. Which is the media used in the confirmed multiple tube fermentation test?
    a. Brilliant green bile
    b. Gypsum
    c. Lauryl tryptose broth
    d. HTH

62. What are the two minimum treatment requirements for surface water?
    a. Flash mix and sedimentation
    b. Filtration and disinfection
    c. Coagulation and flocculation
    d. Sedimentation and filtration

63. What is the clear layer between the sludge and the scum on the top of a basin called?
    a. Supernatant
    b. Schmutzdecke
    c. Biofilm
    d. Metalimnion

64. What is absorption?
    a. When particulates attach to the surface of one another
    b. When a particulate is sucked into another
    c. When particles repel each other
    d. When particles break apart

65. What is a usual characteristic of groundwater?
    a. Lower microbial content
    b. Relatively less turbid
    c. Typically a higher hardness
    d. All the above

66. Which would fall under a secondary standard?
    a. Nitrates
    b. Arsenic
    c. Coliform
    d. Taste and odor

67. What is a water source that is poor in nutrients?
    a. Eutrophic
    b. Mesotrophic
    c. Oligotrophic
    d. Anaerobic

68. A major growth of algae within a reservoir is called an ___ ___.
    a. Stratification
    b. Super concentrated
    c. Algal bloom
    d. Algal season

69. Chlorine combined with organic matter creates ___?
    a. Coliforms
    b. DPD
    c. Hardness
    d. THM's

70. Which is another name for liquid chlorine?
    a. Calcium hypochlorite
    b. Sodium hypochlorite
    c. High test hypochlorite
    d. Alum hypochlorite

71. What is the middle layer of a reservoir called?
    a. Hypolimnion
    b. Metalimnion
    c. Epilimnion
    d. Schmutzdecke

72. Currents within a basin cause ___ ___ problems.
    a. Short circuiting
    b. Lower turbidity
    c. Floc breakthrough
    d. Hard water

73. The efficiency of aeration primarily depends on what factor?
    a. Zeta potential
    b. Organics
    c. Surface contact between air and water
    d. Turbidity

74. The pressure within a chlorine cylinder depends on the ___ of the liquid chlorine.
    a. Turbidity
    b. Hardness
    c. Temperature
    d. P

75. Gas chlorine is fed with a ____.
    a. Hypochlorinator
    b. Chlorinator
    c. Rotameter
    d. Diaphragm

76. The term 'mg/L' can also be expressed as ____.
    a. PPT
    b. MGD
    c. PPM
    d. Gal

77. What is the typical chlorine concentration for disinfecting a new well?
    a. 25 mg/L
    b. 50 mg/L
    c. 75 mg/L
    d. 100 mg/L

78. Corrosive chemicals are usually fed with a ____ pump.
    a. Diaphragm
    b. Turbine
    c. Centrifugal
    d. Rotary

79. A capacity test for a well drilled into an unconfined aquifer usually takes ____ hours.
    a. 24
    b. 32
    c. 48
    d. 72

80. What is the term used to describe cloud formation?
    a. Advection
    b. Condensation
    c. Precipitation
    d. Percolation

81. What is the lowest layer of a reservoir called?
    a. Epilimnion
    b. Metalimnion
    c. Thermocline
    d. Hypolimnion

82. To permit maximum withdrawal when operating a chlorine cylinder, open ___ turn(s).
    a. 4
    b. 3
    c. 2
    d. 1

83. Which chlorine leak kit do you use for a chlorine ton container?
    a. Kit C
    b. Kit A
    c. Kit B
    d. Kit D

84. Chlorine supply lines should be replaced…
    a. Semi-annually
    b. Yearly
    c. Every 2 years
    d. Every 5 years

85. The top valve on a chlorine ton container releases…
    a. Liquid chlorine
    b. Gas chlorine
    c. Sodium hypochlorite
    d. Calcium hypochlorite

86. A storage tank is 50 ft tall and 75 ft in diameter. What is the pressure at the bottom of the tank?
   a. 50 psi
   b. 21.6 psi
   c. 115.5 psi
   d. 144 psi

87. A rectangular reservoir is 100 ft long, 35 ft wide and 10 ft deep. How many pounds of chlorine gas would be needed for a chlorine dose of 60 mg/L?
   a. 60 lbs
   b. 35 lbs
   c. 17.5 lbs
   d. 131 lbs

88. What is the mg/L dose when plant flow is 600 gpm and the feed rate is 75 lbs per day?
   a. 12.3 mg/L
   b. 10.4 mg/L
   c. 17 mg/L
   d. 20 mg/L

89. What is the detention time in hours, if your water tank is 25 ft tall, 49 ft wide, 40 ft long and flow is 2.1 MGD?
   a. 4.19 hours
   b. 5.2 hours
   c. 3.8 hours
   d. 4.3 hours

90. How many pounds of 12.5% sodium hypochlorite do you need to make 520 pounds of 6% chlorine solution?
   a. 320 lbs
   b. 369.8 lbs
   c. 249.6 lbs
   d. 290 lbs

91. Convert 7 cubic ft/ second to MGD.
    a. 4.524 MGD
    b. 4.736 MGD
    c. 7.48 MGD
    d. 7 MGD

92. A rectangular basin is 40 ft wide, 12ft deep and 1 mile long. How many pounds of chlorine gas is needed for a dose of 15 ppm?
    a. 2,371.56 lbs
    b. 1760.09 lbs
    c. 317.05 lbs
    d. 260 lbs

93. If a treatment plant serves 43,000 people, and each person uses 75 gallons of water per day, how long would five 150 lb chlorine gas cylinders last? Assuming the chlorine dose is 3.8 mg/L.
    a. 4.78 days
    b. 6.2 days
    c. 7.34 days
    d. 8.39 days

94. What is the velocity of water in an 8 inch pipe with a flow of 1,200 gpm?
    a. 57.23 ft/sec
    b. 7.63 ft/sec
    c. 6.86 ft/sec
    d. 8.96 ft/sec

95. A 15 MGD plant requires a dose of 10 mg/L of 12% sodium hypochlorite, which weighs 9.257 lbs/gal. How much GPD is required?
    a. 135.03 gal/day
    b. 1,226 gal/day
    c. 150.56 gal/day
    d. 1,126.17 gal/day

96. If 62 lbs of chlorine gas is used with a dosage of 3.2 mg/L, what is the plant's MGD?
   a. 17.376 MGD
   b. 2.323 MGD
   c. 3.232 MGD
   d. 19.375 MGD

97. Convert 5 MGD to cubic ft/ second.
   a. 57.87 cubic ft/sec
   b. 6.94 cubic ft/sec
   c. 8.63 cubic ft/sec
   d. 7.74 cubic ft/sec

98. What is the velocity of water in a 6 inch pipe with a flow rate of 1800 gpm?
   a. 2.73 ft/sec
   b. 2.45 ft/sec
   c. 20.43 ft/sec
   d. 15.92 ft/sec

99. What is the PSI at the bottom of a cylindrical storage container 80 ft tall, 22ft in diameter, and half full?
   a. 17.32 psi
   b. 4.63 psi
   c. 34.63 psi
   d. 38.61 psi

100. What is the chlorine concentration in a cylindrical tank with a diameter of 35 ft and a height of 30 ft, and 15 pounds of 65% calcium hypochlorite is used?
   a. 3.52 mg/L
   b. 5.42 mg/L
   c. 4.52 mg/L
   d. 8.34 mg/L

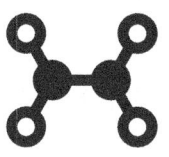

PRACTICE EXAM #2

1. The drop in water level in a well, tank, or reservoir is called __?
    a. Residual
    b. Depth
    c. Drawdown
    d. Water table

2. What is a positively charged ion called?
    a. Colloid
    b. Cation
    c. Neutral
    d. Anion

3. What is a device used to disperse a chemical solution into water being treated?
    a. Lantern ring
    b. Baylis
    c. Centrifugal pump
    d. Ejector

4. Reservoirs and lakes that contain moderate quantities of nutrients are called ____?
    a. Mesotrophic
    b. Eutrophic
    c. Littoral
    d. Oligotrophic

5. The study of fluid in motion is called __?
    a. Waterology
    b. Fluidics
    c. Water physics
    d. Hydraulics

6. What houses the packing and lantern ring in a centrifugal pump?
    a. Outer casing
    b. Stuffing box
    c. Mechanical seal
    d. Inner seal

7. What is the total concentration of chlorine in water, including the combined and free available chlorine called?
    a. Free total chlorine
    b. Combined total chlorine
    c. Chloramine
    d. Total chlorine

8. Who assures safe and healthful working conditions for workers by setting and enforcing standards?
    a. OSHA
    b. NIOSH
    c. CHEMTREC
    d. CHLOREP

9. What happens at the breakpoint of chlorination?
    a. Formation of chloramines
    b. Formation of free available chlorine
    c. Chlorine and chlororganics are partly destroyed
    d. Chlorine is reduced by reducing compounds

10. The capacity of water to neutralize acids is called ___?
    a. Acidic
    b. Neutrality
    c. Alkalinity
    d. Basic

11. The cloudy appearance of water due to suspended matter is called ___?
    a. Appearance
    b. True color
    c. Turbidity
    d. Colloidal

12. The energy lost by water flowing in a pipe, channel, or media is called ___ ___?
    a. Head loss
    b. Rate of loss
    c. Pressure decrease
    d. Drawdown

13. Alum works best in a pH range of what?
    a. 4.2 to 5.5
    b. 5.8 to 8.5
    c. 9.0 to 11.2
    d. 12 to 14

14. Which constituents can cause a discoloring of laundry and can leave stains in fixtures?
    a. Calcium and magnesium
    b. Chlorine and chloramines
    c. Humic and fulvic acids
    d. Iron and manganese

15. Repeat samples for a positive coliform sample need to be taken within ___ hours.
    a. 12
    b. 36
    c. 72
    d. 24

16. Which is the correct laboratory procedure?
    a. Add water to acid
    b. Pour water and acid together at the same time
    c. Add acid to water
    d. Add water to chemicals

17. Which of the following pH ranges is considered basic?
    a. 8-14
    b. 6-7
    c. 1-6
    d. 1-3

18. Why is fluoride injected into drinking water?
    a. Prevent galvanic corrosion
    b. Reduce tooth decay
    c. Act as a filter aid
    d. Increase alkalinity

19. How many days does the water system have to notify the state primacy agency of full compliance with the public notification rule?
    a. 7 days
    b. 12 days
    c. 10 days
    d. 20 days

20. Which of the following is a sequestering agent?
    a. Sodium polyphosphate
    b. Trichloroethylene
    c. Sodium hypochlorite
    d. Soda ash

21. Which is the correct written form of calcium carbonate?
    a. CaCO2
    b. CaCO3
    c. CaCO4
    d. CaCO5

22. Where should a sample for lead and copper be taken at?
    a. Farthest point in distribution system
    b. At plant effluent
    c. Raw water intake
    d. Customer's tap

23. What is the log removal for giardia?
    a. 99.99%
    b. 9%
    c. 99%
    d. 99.9%

24. What are the two most commonly used metals for sacrificial anodes?
    a. Magnesium and zinc
    b. Gold and silver
    c. Calcium and manganese
    d. Lead and copper

25. How does GAC primarily remove contaminants from the water?
    a. Straining
    b. Adsorption
    c. Titration
    d. Absorption

26. A well's ___ determines how much water it can hold.
    a. Density
    b. Turbidity
    c. Porosity
    d. Layers

27. What causes alkalinity and pH to drop when added to water?
    a. Carbon dioxide
    b. Soda ash
    c. Lime
    d. Caustic soda

28. What is the process of vertical mixing within a lake or reservoir to eliminate separate layers called?
    a. Thermocline
    b. Stratification
    c. Salinization
    d. Destratification

29. What is a safe dosage of copper sulfate if fish in the reservoir are a concern?
    a. 2.5 mg/L
    b. 0.5 mg/L
    c. 5.0 mg/L
    d. 1.0 mg/L

30. Which is the correct chemical formula for hydrated lime?
    a. Na(OH)2
    b. Cl(OH)2
    c. Ca(OH)2
    d. Ca(CO)2

31. When should phosphate used for sequestering iron be added?
    a. After chlorine
    b. At plant influent
    c. Before chlorine
    d. At flash mix

32. When water is softened through a zeolite ion exchange process, which is substituted for the calcium and magnesium ions?
    a. Sodium
    b. Lead
    c. Iron
    d. Copper

33. Viruses are the ____ of pathogens.
    a. Largest
    b. Smallest
    c. Medium
    d. Most settleable

34. How many coliform positive samples can you have if your system collects fewer than 40 samples per month?
    a. 5
    b. 1%
    c. 1
    d. 5%

35. What does sodium thiosulfate do?
    a. Removes turbidity
    b. Kills coliform
    c. Acts as a filter aid
    d. Neutralizes chlorine

36. What is the main use of Alum?
    a. Oxidant
    b. Coagulant
    c. Disinfectant
    d. Strainer

37. Which is the most powerful oxidant?
    a. Oxygen
    b. UV
    c. Ozone
    d. Potassium permanganate

38. Which is the correct order of tests in the multiple tube fermentation method?
    a. Presumptive, confirmed, completed
    b. Completed, confirmed, presumptive
    c. Presumptive, confirmed, conclusion
    d. Presumptive, completed, confirmed

39. Chlorine has the most trouble inactivating ___.
    a. Viruses
    b. Giardia
    c. Cryptosporidium
    d. Algae

40. When collecting a first draw sample for lead and copper, how long must the tap be unused?
    a. 6 days
    b. 6 hours
    c. 6 minutes
    d. 6 weeks

41. Where do volatile organic chemicals usually come from?
    a. Industrial solvents
    b. Cleaning solutions
    c. Gas additives
    d. All the above

42. Which of the following raises alkalinity?
    a. Calcium hypochlorite
    b. Ferric sulfate
    c. Chlorine gas
    d. Carbon dioxide

43. What is the action level for lead?
    a. 0.05 mg/L
    b. 0.3 mg/L
    c. 0.015 mg/L
    d. 1.3 mg/L

44. Which is a condition that occurs when a pump is ran too fast and you hear a pinging noise?
    a. Capitulation
    b. Drawdown
    c. Overdraw
    d. Cavitation

45. A seal placed on a pump shaft to prevent water from leaking along the shaft is called?
    a. Mechanical seal
    b. Lantern ring
    c. Packing gland
    d. Total seal

46. What is the name of an assessment of the entire system to determine where weaknesses would lie if a given disaster were to take place?
    a. Sanitary survey
    b. Vulnerability assessment
    c. Confidence report
    d. Sanitary assessment

47. Red water problems can usually be attributed to ___?
    a. Lead
    b. Manganese
    c. Iron
    d. Copper

48. Black water problems can usually be attributed to ___?
    a. Magnesium
    b. Lead
    c. Manganese
    d. Chlorine

49. You use a chlorine repair kit _ to repair 150 lb chlorine cylinders.
    a. C
    b. B
    c. D
    d. A

50. Water with a concentration of calcium and magnesium less than ___ mg/L is usually considered soft
    a. 160
    b. 100
    c. 60
    d. 210

51. Water becomes scale forming after what point on the Langelier Index?
    a. -8
    b. 1
    c. -4
    d. -1

52. Which of the following does not leave a detectable residual?
    a. Chlorine
    b. Chlorine dioxide
    c. UV
    d. Chloramine

53. Nitrates in the water can cause what?
    a. Methemoglobinemia
    b. Giardiasis
    c. Trihalomethanes
    d. Salmonella

54. Which are early warning signs of nitrification?
    a. Decrease in ammonia
    b. Decrease in chlorine
    c. Decrease in pH
    d. All the above

55. The MCL for positive coliform samples is based on ___?
    a. Population
    b. Tank-sites
    c. Services
    d. Well-sites

56. What is the water right given to be able to divert water upstream?
    a. Riparian
    b. Prescriptive
    c. Appropriative
    d. Doctrine

57. Water that falls back to the ground in the form of rain, hail, or snow is called ___?
    a. Precipitation
    b. Permeation
    c. Percolation
    d. Condensation

58. The depressed water surface around a well while it's running is called what?
    a. Static water level
    b. Drawdown
    c. Cone of depression
    d. Yield

59. Waters with a low pH tend to cause what kind of problems?
    a. Odor
    b. Coliform
    c. Corrosion
    d. Taste

60. Hydrogen sulfide does what to water?
    a. Releases an odor
    b. Scale forming
    c. Improves coagulation
    d. Turbidity

61. Which is a check valve located at the bottom of a pump to hold the prime?
    a. Gate valve
    b. Foot valve
    c. Butterfly valve
    d. Pressure reducing valve

62. Which of the following is an effect of pump/motor misalignment?
    a. Excessive noise and vibration
    b. Bearing or seal failure
    c. Overheating
    d. All the above

63. Which is the immediately dangerous to life and health limit of chlorine gas?
    a. 10 ppm
    b. 0.005 ppm
    c. 0.5 ppm
    d. 1 ppm

64. Which chlorine repair kit do you use for a rail car repair?
    a. Kit B
    b. Kit C
    c. Kit A
    d. Kit D

65. What is the media used in the confirmed test of the multiple tube fermentation method?
    a. Lauryl tryptose broth
    b. Blue agar
    c. Colilert agent
    d. Brilliant green bile broth

66. What is the formulation of rust inside metallic pipe called?
    a. Tuberculation
    b. Permeation
    c. Condensation
    d. Turbidity

67. Total alkalinity should be measured every how many hours for corrosion control purposes?
    a. 72 hours
    b. 4 hours
    c. 8 hours
    d. 12 hours

68. How long should a treatment plant always keep a chemical supply on hand?
    a. 7 days
    b. 60 days
    c. 24 days
    d. 30 days

69. Which is the disinfection procedure of passing air through a electrical current?
    a. UV
    b. Ozone
    c. Potassium permanganate
    d. Chlorination

70. Which of the following is a byproduct of using ozone for disinfection?
    a. Bromate
    b. Trichloroethylene
    c. Trihalomethane
    d. Haloacetic acid

71. Groundwater under the influence of surface water should be treated as?
    a. Dangerous
    b. Groundwater
    c. Surface water
    d. Waste

72. What consists of a rotating set of vanes that force water through a pump?
    a. Diffuser
    b. Impeller
    c. Eductor
    d. Coupling shaft

73. The concentration of chlorine in the water after the demand is met is called?
    a. Chlorine demand
    b. Combined chlorine
    c. Chlorine dose
    d. Chlorine residual

74. The addition of hydrogen, removal of oxygen, or addition of electrons is called?
    a. Reduction
    b. Addition
    c. Oxidation
    d. Aeration

75. Which type of chlorine residual test is typically done in the laboratory?
    a. MTF
    b. DPD
    c. Amperometric titration
    d. MPN

76. Particulates that clump together are called what?
    a. Coagulant
    b. Flocs
    c. Colloids
    d. DBP's

77. Which procedure simulates the water treatment plant processes to determine optimum coagulant dosages?
    a. Colilert test
    b. Jar Test
    c. MTF test
    d. DPD test

78. Sodium aluminate ____ coagulation when used with alum.
    a. Slows
    b. Decreases
    c. Neutralizes
    d. Improves

79. Very small particles that resist settling are called?
    a. Colloids
    b. Settleable solids
    c. Flocs
    d. Clumps

80. Deposits of rust on metallic pipe can also be called?
    a. Accumulates
    b. Ferric hydroxide
    c. Organic hydroxide
    d. Ferrous hydroxide

81. Warmer water temperature typically ____ coagulation, flocculation, sedimentation and filtration.
    a. Improves
    b. Slows
    c. Neutralizes
    d. Decreases

82. The land area that contributes to the drainage or catchment area above a specific point on a stream or river is called?
    a. Easement
    b. Channel
    c. Watershed
    d. Radius of influence

83. Where are coagulants rapidly mixed during the treatment process?
    a. Fast mixer
    b. Radial mixer
    c. Flash mixer
    d. Charged mixer

84. Which of the following is the most effective way to remove TDS?
    a. Ozone
    b. Reverse osmosis
    c. Enhanced coagulation
    d. Conventional filtration

85. Which of the following is not considered a free chlorine residual?
    a. Hypochlorous acid
    b. Chlorine
    c. Hypochlorite Ion
    d. Monochloramine

86. What is the unit filter run volume of a filtration bed that is 40 feet in length, 15 feet in width, and treats 4 million gallons of water per filter run?
    a. 2,000 gal/sq.ft
    b. 6,667 gal/sq.ft
    c. 3,500 gal/sq.ft
    d. 1,500 gal/sq.ft

87. A 75 foot high storage tank measures 35 feet long and 80 feet wide. How much chlorine is needed for a dose of 10 mg/L?
    a. 131 lbs
    b. 56 lbs
    c. 15.7 lbs
    d. 146.07 lbs

88. A 150 foot high cylindrical storage tank has a diameter of 40 feet. How much chlorine is needed for a dose of 15 mg/L?
    a. 21.14 lbs
    b. 158.12 lbs
    c. 141.82 lbs
    d. 176.3 lbs

89. A well is pumped at a rate of 1,890 gpm. You are using 65% available calcium hypochlorite. How many pounds per day of chlorine is needed for a dose of 15 mg/L?
    a. 232 lbs
    b. 523.8 lbs
    c. 459 lbs
    d. 340.47 lbs

90. What is the area of a pipe if 8 cu ft/sec of water is passing through the pipe at a rate of 4 ft/sec?
    a. 2 sq.ft
    b. 8 sq.ft
    c. 6 sq.ft
    d. 10 sq.ft

91. What is the mg/L dose when plant flow is 650 gpm and a feed rate of 70 lbs per day?
   a. 3.36 mg/L
   b. 6.65 mg/L
   c. 8.97 mg/L
   d. 4.57 mg/L

92. The iron concentration in your water is 32 mg/L and the daily flow is 1900 gpm. If the plant removes 85% of the iron, how many lbs of iron are removed daily?
   a. 480.82 lbs
   b. 403.44 lbs
   c. 954.87 lbs
   d. 620.66 lbs

93. Your treatment plant has 4 filter beds that each measure 30 ft long by 40 ft wide. If your flow is 1 MGD, what is the filtration rate in gpm/sq. ft?
   a. 0.36 gpm/sq.ft
   b. 0.14 gpm/sq. ft
   c. 1.02 gpm/sq.ft
   d. 0.44 gpm/sq.ft

94. A 500 gpm pump with a efficiency of 80% and an motor of 90% efficiency are used to lift water 25 feet, 24 hours per day. If the electrical cost is $0.18/kWh, what is the daily electrical cost to run the pump?
   a. $14.12
   b. $7.14
   c. $20.50
   d. $15.72

95. A 12-in water main 1,000-ft long needs to be disinfected. A chlorine dose of 35 mg/L is used for 24 hours. How many gallons of 8% sodium hypochlorite be needed? (Chemical weight is 12 lbs/gal)
   a. 2.24 gallons
   b. 1.79 gallons
   c. 3.24 gallons
   d. 7.19 gallons

96. What is the detention time in hours if your storage tank was 30 ft tall with a diameter of 50 ft and a flow of 4 MGD?
    a. 2.64 hours
    b. 4.26 hours
    c. 3.75 hours
    d. 6.24 hours

97. If a water meter reads 57,000 gallons on the 1st of the month, and then reads 62,000 30 days later, what was the average daily consumption in gallons?
    a. 203 gallons per day
    b. 405.6 gallons per day
    c. 166.7 gallons per day
    d. 676.1 gallons per day

98. How much water is in a basin if 70 lbs of chlorine gas was added to achieve a chlorine dose of 4 mg/L?
    a. 3,050,072 gallons
    b. 2,132,890 gallons
    c. 1,980, 231 gallons
    d. 2,098,321 gallons

99. Raw water flows into the plant through a trapezoidal ditch that measures 16 ft across the top, 14 ft across the bottom, 6 feet deep and 6 miles long. How much water does this ditch hold when full?
    a. 2,851,200 gallons
    b. 52,234,567 gallons
    c. 21,326,976 gallons
    d. 32,196,647 gallons

100. A hypochlorinator feeds a 6% chlorine solution and has a maximum capacity of 7 gph. What is the mg/L dose when plant flow is 300 gpm?
    a. 23.3 mg/L
    b. 51.92 mg/L
    c. 17.89 mg/L
    d. 388.33 mg/L

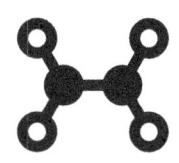

EXAM #1 ANSWER SHEET

1. C	26. D	51. A	76. C
2. B	27. A	52. C	77. B
3. D	28. C	53. D	78. A
4. B	29. D	54. C	79. D
5. A	30. A	55. B	80. B
6. C	31. D	56. B	81. D
7. D	32. C	57. A	82. D
8. C	33. A	58. D	83. C
9. A	34. D	59. C	84. B
10. C	35. B	60. C	85. B
11. D	36. C	61. A	86. B
12. B	37. A	62. B	87. D
13. D	38. D	63. A	88. B
14. B	39. C	64. B	89. A
15. D	40. B	65. D	90. C
16. A	41. D	66. D	91. A
17. C	42. A	67. C	92. A
18. D	43. C	68. C	93. C
19. B	44. B	69. D	94. B
20. A	45. D	70. B	95. D
21. C	46. D	71. B	96. B
22. A	47. B	72. A	97. D
23. B	48. C	73. C	98. C
24. D	49. A	74. C	99. A
25. A	50. B	75. B	100. B

86. A storage tank is 50 ft tall and 75 ft in diameter. What is the pressure at the bottom of the tank?

Psi= (head, ft)
      2.31 ft/psi

Psi= (50, ft)
      2.31 ft/psi

Psi= 21.6

87. A rectangular reservoir is 100 ft long, 35 ft wide and 10 ft deep. How many pounds of chlorine gas would be needed for a chlorine dose of 60 mg/L?

(gas) lbs= Vol, MG x mg/L x 8.34lbs/gal

Vol, rectangular basin, gal= (length, ft) x (width, ft) x (height, ft) x 7.48 gal/cu.ft
         = 100ft x 35ft x 10ft x 7.48
         = 261,800 gallons
           1,000,000
         = 0.2618 MG
(gas) lbs= 0.2618 MG x 60 mg/L x 8.34 lbs/gal
     Lbs= 131

88. What is the mg/L dose when plant flow is 600 gpm and the feed rate is 75 lbs per day?

(Gas) lbs= Vol, MG x mg/L x 8.34 lbs/gal

600 gpm x 1440 min/day = 864,000 gal   Or
                         1,000,000
                       = 0.864 MGD

75 lbs= 0.864 MG x mg/L x 8.34

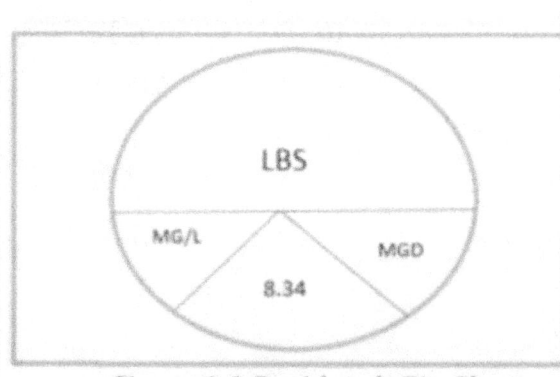

mg/L = 10.4

Figure 1.0 Davidson's Pie Chart

89. What is the detention time in hours, if your water tank is 25 ft tall, 49 ft wide, 40 ft long and flow is 2.1 MGD?

Detention time hours = $\dfrac{\text{vol (cu.ft)} \times 7.48 \text{ gal/cu.ft} \times 24 \text{ hrs/day}}{\text{Gal/day}}$

Vol, cu.ft = 25ft x 49ft x 40ft
= 49,000 cu.ft

2.1 MGD x 1,000,000
= 2,100,000 gal/day

DT, hours = $\dfrac{49,000 \text{ft} \times 7.48 \times 24 \text{ hrs/day}}{2,100,000 \text{ gal/day}}$

= 4.188 hours

90. How many pounds of 12.5% sodium hypochlorite do you need to make 520 pounds of 6% chlorine solution?

$C_1V_1 = C_2V_2$ Rewrite formula as: $V_1 = \dfrac{C_2V_2}{C_1}$

$V_1 = \dfrac{6\% \times 520 \text{ lbs}}{12.5\%}$

V_1 = 249.6 lbs

91. Convert 7 cubic ft/ second to MGD.

7 cu.ft x 60 sec x 60 min x 24 hrs
= 604,800 cu.ft/day

604,800 cu.ft/day x 7.48 gal/cu.ft
= 4,523,904 gal/day

$\dfrac{4,523,904 \text{ gal/day}}{1,000,000}$ = 4.524 MGD

92. A rectangular basin is 40 ft wide, 12ft deep and 1 mile long. How many pounds of chlorine gas is needed for a dose of 15 ppm?

(Gas) lbs = Vol, MG x mg/L x 8.34 lbs/gal   1 mile= 5280 ft

Vol, rectangular basin, gal= (length, ft) x (width, ft) x (height, ft) x 7.48 gal/cu.ft
    = 5280 ft x 40 ft x 12 ft x 7.48 gal/cu.ft
    = 18,957,312 gallons

$$\frac{18,957,312 \text{ gal}}{1,000,000} = 18.9573 \text{ MGD}$$

Lbs = 18.9573 MG x 15 mg/L x 8.34 lbs/gal
    = 2,371.56 lbs

93. If a treatment plant serves 43,000 people, and each person uses 75 gallons of water per day, how long would five 150 lb chlorine gas cylinders last? Assuming the chlorine dose is 3.8 mg/L.

75 gal/day x 43,000 people = 3,225,000 gal

$$\frac{3,225,000 \text{ gal}}{1,000,000} = 3.225 \text{ MGD}$$

Lbs= MGD x mg/L x 8.34 lbs/gal   5 cylinders x 150 lbs/cylinder
    = 3.225 MGD x 3.8 mg/L x 8.34 lbs/gal   = 750 lbs
Lbs= 102.21

$$\frac{750 \text{ lbs}}{102.21 \text{ lbs}} = 7.34 \text{ days}$$

94. What is the velocity of water in an 8 inch pipe with a flow of 1,200 gpm?

V, ft/sec = Q, cu.ft/sec
                A, sq.ft   8 in = 0.6666 ft

A= 0.785 x 0.6666 ft x 0.6666 ft
  = 0.35 sq.ft

Q= 1,200 gpm ÷ 60 sec ÷ 7.48 gal/cu.ft
  = 2.67 cu.ft/sec

V= Q ÷ A
  = 2.67 cu.ft/sec ÷ 0.35 sq.ft
  = 7.63 ft/sec

95. A 15 MGD plant requires a dose of 10 mg/L of 12% sodium hypochlorite, which weighs 9.257 lbs/gal. How much GPD is required?

Liquid, gal = (vol, MG) x (mg/L) x 8.34 lbs/gal
              (% strength /100) x chemical wt. (lbs/gal)

           = 15 MG x 10 mg/L x 8.34 lbs/gal
                  (0.12) x 9.257 lbs/gal

           = 1,126.17 gal/day

96. If 62 lbs of chlorine gas is used with a dosage of 3.2 mg/L, what is the plant's MGD?

Lbs= Vol, MG x mg/L x 8.34 lbs/gal

62 lbs= MG x 3.2 mg/L x 8.34 lbs/gal

=   62lbs
    26.688 = 2.323 MGD

97. Convert 5 MGD to cubic ft/ second.

5 MGD x 1,000,000 = 5,000,000 gal

5,000,000 gal ÷ 7.48 gal/cu.ft
= 669,449.198 cu.ft/day

669,449.198 cu.ft/day ÷ 86,400 sec/day
= 7.74 cu.ft/sec

98. What is the velocity of water in a 6 inch pipe with a flow rate of 1800 gpm?

V, ft/sec = Q, cu.ft/sec
          A, sq.ft   6 in= 0.5 ft

A= 0.785 x 0.5 ft x 0.5 ft
  = 0.19625 sq.ft

Q= 1800gpm ÷ 60 sec ÷ 7.48 gal/cu.ft
  = 4.01 cu.ft/sec

V= 4.01 cu.ft/sec
    0.19625 sq.ft
 = 20.43 ft/sec

99. What is the PSI at the bottom of a cylindrical storage container 80 ft tall, 22ft in diameter, and half full?

PSI= (head, ft)
     2.31 ft/psi   80 ft ÷ 2 = 40 ft

  = (40 ft)   = 17.32 psi
    2.31 ft/psi

100. What is the chlorine concentration in a cylindrical tank with a diameter of 35 ft and a height of 30 ft, and 15 pounds of 65% calcium hypochlorite is used?

HTH (lbs) = (vol, MG) x (mg/L) x (8.34 lbs/gal)
                    (% strength /100)

Vol, cylinder, gal = 0.785 x 35 ft x 35 ft x 30 ft x 7.48 gal/cu.ft
            = 215,788.65 gal

215,788.65 gal ÷ 1,000,000
= 0.21579 MGD

15 lbs = (0.21579 MG) x (mg/L) x (8.34 lbs/gal)
                    (0.65)

15 lbs x (0.65) = (0.21579 MG) x (mg/L) x (8.34 lbs/gal)   ~~(0.65)~~
                                    ~~(0.65)~~

9.75 lbs = (0.21579 MG) x (mg/L) x (8.34 lbs/gal)

9.75 lbs = 1.7997 x mg/L

9.75 lbs = ~~1.7997~~ x mg/L
 1.7997   ~~1.7997~~

Mg/L = 5.42

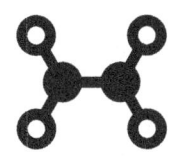

EXAM # 2 ANSWER SHEET

1. C	26. C	51. B	76. B
2. B	27. A	52. C	77. B
3. D	28. D	53. A	78. D
4. A	29. B	54. D	79. A
5. D	30. C	55. A	80. B
6. B	31. C	56. B	81. A
7. D	32. A	57. A	82. C
8. A	33. B	58. C	83. C
9. B	34. C	59. C	84. B
10. C	35. D	60. A	85. D
11. C	36. B	61. B	86. B
12. A	37. C	62. D	87. A
13. B	38. A	63. A	88. D
14. D	39. C	64. B	89. B
15. D	40. B	65. D	90. A
16. C	41. D	66. A	91. C
17. A	42. A	67. C	92. D
18. B	43. C	68. D	93. B
19. C	44. D	69. B	94. A
20. A	45. A	70. A	95. B
21. B	46. B	71. C	96. A
22. D	47. C	72. B	97. C
23. D	48. C	73. D	98. D
24. A	49. D	74. A	99. C
25. B	50. C	75. C	100. A

86. What is the unit filter run volume of a filtration bed that is 40 feet in length, 15 feet in width, and treats 4 million gallons of water?

UFRV= (gals produced in a filter run)
 (Filter area, sq.ft)

Filter area, sq.ft= 40 ft x 15 ft
 = 600 sq.ft

= 4,000,000 gal
 600 sq.ft

UFRV= 6,667 gal/sq.ft

87. A 75 foot high storage tank measures 35 feet long and 80 feet wide. How much chlorine is needed for a dose of 10 mg/L?

Lbs= MGD x mg/L x 8.34 lbs/gal

Vol, rectangular basin, gal= 75 ft x 35 ft x 80 ft x 7.48 gal/cu.ft
 = 1,570,800 gal
 1,000,000   = 1.5708 MGD

Lbs= 1.5708 MGD x 10 mg/L x 8.34 lbs/gal
 = 131 lbs

88. A 150 foot high cylindrical storage tank has a diameter of 40 feet. How much chlorine is needed for a dose of 15 mg/L?

Lbs= MGD x mg/L x 8.34 lbs/gal

Vol, cylindrical tank, gal= 0.785 x (dia, ft) x (dia, ft) x (height, ft) x 7.48 gal/cu.ft
 = 0.785 x 40 ft x 40 ft x 150 ft x 7.48 gal/cu.ft
 = 1,409,232 gal
 1,000,000   =1.409 MGD

Lbs= 1.409 MGD x 15 mg/L x 8.34 lbs/gal
 = 176.3 lbs

89. A well is pumped at a rate of 1,890 gpm. You are using 65% available calcium hypochlorite. How many pounds per day of chlorine is needed for a dose of 15 mg/L?

HTH (lbs)= MGD x mg/L x 8.34 lbs/gal
                (% strength/ 100)

1890 gpm x 1440 min/day
= 2,721,600 gal
  1,000,000   = 2.7216 MGD

Lbs= 2.7216 MGD x 15 mg/L x 8.34 lbs/gal
                0.65

= 523.8 lbs

90. What is the area of a pipe if 8 cu ft/sec of water is passing through the pipe at a rate of 4 ft/sec?

A= Q, cu.ft/sec ÷ V, ft/sec

A= 8 cu.ft/sec ÷ 4 ft/sec
 = 2 sq.ft

91. What is the mg/L dose when plant flow is 650 gpm and a feed rate of 70 lbs per day?

Lbs= MGD x mg/L x 8.34 lbs/gal

650 gpm x 1440 min/day
= 936,000 gal
  1,000,000   = 0.936 MGD

70 lbs= 0.936 MGD x mg/L x 8.34 lbs/gal

70 lbs= ~~7.806~~ x mg/L
7.806   ~~7.806~~

Mg/L= 8.97

92. The iron concentration in your water is 32 mg/L and the daily flow is 1900 gpm. If the plant removes 85% of the iron, how many lbs of iron are removed daily?

Lbs= MGD x mg/L x 8.34 lbs/gal x (% /100)

1900 gpm x 1440 min/day
= 2,736,000 gal
1,000,000   = 2.736 MGD

Lbs= 2.736 MGD x 32 mg/L x 8.34 lbs/gal x (0.85)
    = 620.66 lbs

93. Your treatment plant has 4 filter beds that each measure 30 ft long by 40 ft wide. If your flow is 1 MGD, what is the filtration rate in gpm/sq. ft?

Filtration Rate= Filter production, gallons/day
                (Filter area, sq.ft) x (1440 min/day)

1 MGD x 1,000,000
= 1,000,000 gal

Filter Area, sq.ft= 30 ft x 40 ft x 4 filter beds
                  = 4,800 sq.ft

Filtration Rate= 1,000,000 gallons
                4,800 sq.ft x 1440 min/day

               = 0.14 gpm/sq.ft

94. A 500 gpm pump with a efficiency of 80% and an motor of 90% efficiency are used to lift water 25 feet, 24 hours per day. If the electrical cost is $0.18/kWh, what is the daily electrical cost to run the pump?

Motor Hp= (Gpm) x (Total head, ft)
          (3,960) x (pump % eff.) x (motor % eff.)

= 500 gpm x 25 ft   = 4.38 Hp
  3960 x 0.80 x 0.90

Cost $= (Hp) x (0.746 Kw/Hp) x (operating hours) x (cents/Kw-hr)
     = 4.38 Hp x 0.746 Kw/Hp x 24 hrs x $0.18/kWh   = $14.12

95. A 12 inch water main 1,000 feet long needs to be disinfected. A chlorine dose of 35 mg/L is used for 24 hours. How many gallons of 8% sodium hypochlorite be needed? (SW= 12 lbs/gal)

Gal= $\dfrac{\text{MGD x mg/L x 8.34 lbs/gal}}{(\text{\% strength}/100) \text{ x (chem wt, lbs/gal)}}$ 12 in= 1 ft

Vol, cylinder, gal= 0.785 x (dia, ft) x (dia, ft) x (length, ft) x 7.48 gal/cu.ft
  = 0.785 x 1 ft x 1 ft x 1,000 ft x 7.48 gal/cu.ft
  = <u>5,871.8 gal</u>
     1,000,000 = 0.0058718 MGD

Gal= $\dfrac{0.0058718 \text{ MGD x 35 mg/L x 8.34 lbs/gal}}{(0.08) \text{ x (12 lbs/gal)}}$

= 1.79 gallon

96. What is the detention time in hours if your storage tank was 30 ft tall with a diameter of 50 ft and a flow of 4 MGD?

Detention Time hours= $\dfrac{(\text{vol, cu.ft}) \text{ x (7.48 gal/cu.ft) x (24 hrs/day)}}{\text{Gal/day}}$

Vol, cylinder, cu.ft= 0.785 x (dia,ft) x (dia, ft) x height, ft   4 MGD x 1,000,000
  = 0.785 x 50 ft x 50 ft x 30 ft   = 4,000,000 gallons
  = 58,875 cu.ft

DT hours= $\dfrac{58,875 \text{ cu.ft x 7.48 gal/cu.ft x 24 hrs/day}}{4,000,000 \text{ gallons}}$

= 2.64 hours

97. If a water meter reads 57,000 gallons on the 1st of the month, and then reads 62,000 30 days later, what was the average daily consumption in gallons?

GPD= (meter 2 read) - (meter 1 read)
             Days

= 62,000 - 57,000
        30

= 166.7 gal/day

98. How much water is in a basin if 70 lbs of chlorine gas was added to achieve a chlorine dose of 4 mg/L?

Lbs= MGD x mg/L x 8.34 lbs/gal

70 lbs= MGD x 4 mg/L x 8.34 lbs/gal

70 lbs= MGD x ~~33.36~~
33.36   ~~33.36~~

MGD= 2.09832134 x 1,000,000 = 2,098,321 gallons

99. Raw water flows into the plant through a trapezoidal ditch that measures 16 ft across the top, 14 ft across the bottom, 6 feet deep and 6 miles long. How much water does this ditch hold when full?

Vol, trapezoidal basin, gal= 1/2(top,ft - bottom,ft) x height, ft x length, ft x 7.48 gal/cu.ft

= (16 ft + 14 ft) x (6 ft) x (31,680 ft) x 7.48 gal/cu.ft   1 mile= 5280 ft
         2

= (15) x 6 ft x 31,680 ft x 7.48 gal/cu.ft

= 21,326,976 gallons

100. A hypochlorinator feeds a 6% chlorine solution and has a maximum capacity of 7 gph. What is the mg/L dose when plant flow is 300 gpm?

7 gph x 24 hours= 168 gal/day

168 gal/day x 8.34 lbs/gal = 1,401.12 lbs/day

1,401.12 lbs/day x 0.06= 84.07 lbs/day

Lbs= MGD x mg/L x 8.34 lbs/gal

84.07 lbs= 0.432 MGD x mg/L x 8.34 lbs/gal

$\dfrac{84.07 \text{ lbs}}{3.60288} = \dfrac{3.60288 \times mg/L}{3.60288}$

Mg/L= 23.3

300 gpm x 1440 min/day
= 432,000 gal ÷ 1,000,000
= 0.432 MGD

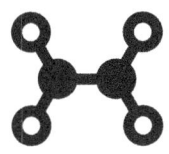

ABOUT THE AUTHOR

I come from a small farm town in Southern California. Since a young age, I have always wanted to follow in the footsteps of my dad and grandpa who both worked in the water industry through their careers. Through determination to succeed, I am now the third generation of my family who works in the water industry. I studied hard enough to get my distribution grade 2 and treatment grade 2 water certifications right out of high school and managed to get a job working for my local utility. I have developed a real passion for the water industry and love every second I get working in it, along with teaching and helping others get their certifications like I have. I take great pride knowing that I serve my community by helping to provide a clean and safe drinking water. The world will always need qualified operators to deliver clean drinking water that is safe. I am proud to be one of them.

Made in the USA
Las Vegas, NV
11 September 2023